Crochet for Beginners

The Definitive Step-by-Step Guide with Pictures, Illustrations, and Pattern Ideas to Easily Learn Crocheting and Effortlessly Become a Pro

Lorena Jackson

© Copyright 2023 - All rights reserved.

The content contained within this book may not be reproduced, duplicated or transmitted without direct written permission from the author or the publisher. Under no circumstances will any blame or legal responsibility be held against the publisher, or author, for any damages, reparation, or monetary loss due to the information contained within this book. Either directly or indirectly.

Legal Notice:

This book is copyright protected. This book is only for personal use. You cannot amend, distribute, sell, use, quote or paraphrase any part, or the content within this book, without the consent of the author or publisher.

Disclaimer Notice:

Please note the information contained within this document is for educational and entertainment purposes only. All effort has been executed to present accurate, up to date, and reliable, complete information. No warranties of any kind are declared or implied. Readers acknowledge that the author is not engaging in the rendering of legal, financial, medical or professional advice. The content within this book has been derived from various sources. Please consult a licensed professional before attempting any techniques outlined in this book.

By reading this document, the reader agrees that under no circumstances is the author responsible for any losses, direct or indirect, which are incurred as a result of the use of information contained within this document, including, but not limited to, errors, omissions, or inaccuracies.

Contents

Introduction 5

Chapter 1: A Complete Overview 7

    What Is Crochet? 8

    History Of Crochet 9

    Difference Between Crochet And Weaving 10

    Difference Between Crochet And Tatting 11

    What Can You Make With Crochet 12

Chapter 2: Choosing The Perfect Crocheting Supplies 15

    Crochet hooks: 18

    Yarn 22

    Yarn needle: 25

    Stitch markers: 26

    Other Tools 27

Chapter 3: How To Understand and Read Crochet Patterns 29

    Gauge 31

Chapter 4: Different Basic Stitches Of Crochet 33

    Slip Stitch or Slipknot 34

    Ch-Chain Stitch : 35

    Single crochet: 36

    Half Double crochet: 37

    Double crochet: 38

    Treble Crochet : 39

Chapter 5: Crochet For Right And Left Handers 41

Chapter 6: How To Avoid Most Common Mistakes 45

Chapter 7: Best Tips And Tricks For Newbies 53

Chapter 9: Best Crochet Pattern Ideas And Projects 55

    Crochet Sweater Pattern 57

    Crocheted Hand Mittens 60

    Crochet Cap 62

    Crochet Shawl 64

    Two Colored Crochet Bag 66

    Crochet Cardigan 68

    Colorful Crochet Socks: 71

    Crochet Blanket 74

    Crochet Dishcloth 76

    Crochet Headband 78

    Crochet Granny Square 80

    Crochet Beanie Cap Pattern 83

    Crochet Griddle Stitch Scarf Pattern 86

    Baby Crochet Blanket Pattern 88

    Crochet Bracelet Pattern 90

    Crochet Gloves Pattern 92

    Crochet Crop Top Pattern 94

    Crochet Cowl Pattern 97

Chapter 10: FAQ 99

Conclusion 103

Introduction

Crocheting is a wonderful craft that has been enjoyed by people for centuries. With just a hook and some yarn, you can create a variety of beautiful items, from cozy blankets and warm scarves to fashionable accessories and cute amigurumi toys. If you're new to crocheting, don't worry! One such resource is this Crochet for beginners, which can provide you with step-by-step Directions and helpful tips to guide you. In this crochet for beginners guide book, you can expect to find information on the crochet stitches as well as how to read crochet patterns and charts. You'll also learn about different types of yarn and hooks, and their types. This book will also include a variety of beginner-friendly patterns, ranging from simple washcloths and dishcloths to more complex items like blankets and hats. These patterns will allow you to practice your new skills and create some beautiful items that you can be proud of. Whether you're interested in crocheting as a relaxing hobby, or you're hoping to create some handmade gifts for your loved ones, a crochet for beginners book is a great place to start. With a bit of patience and practice, you'll be on your way to creating beautiful crocheted items in no time!

Chapter 1:
A Complete Overview

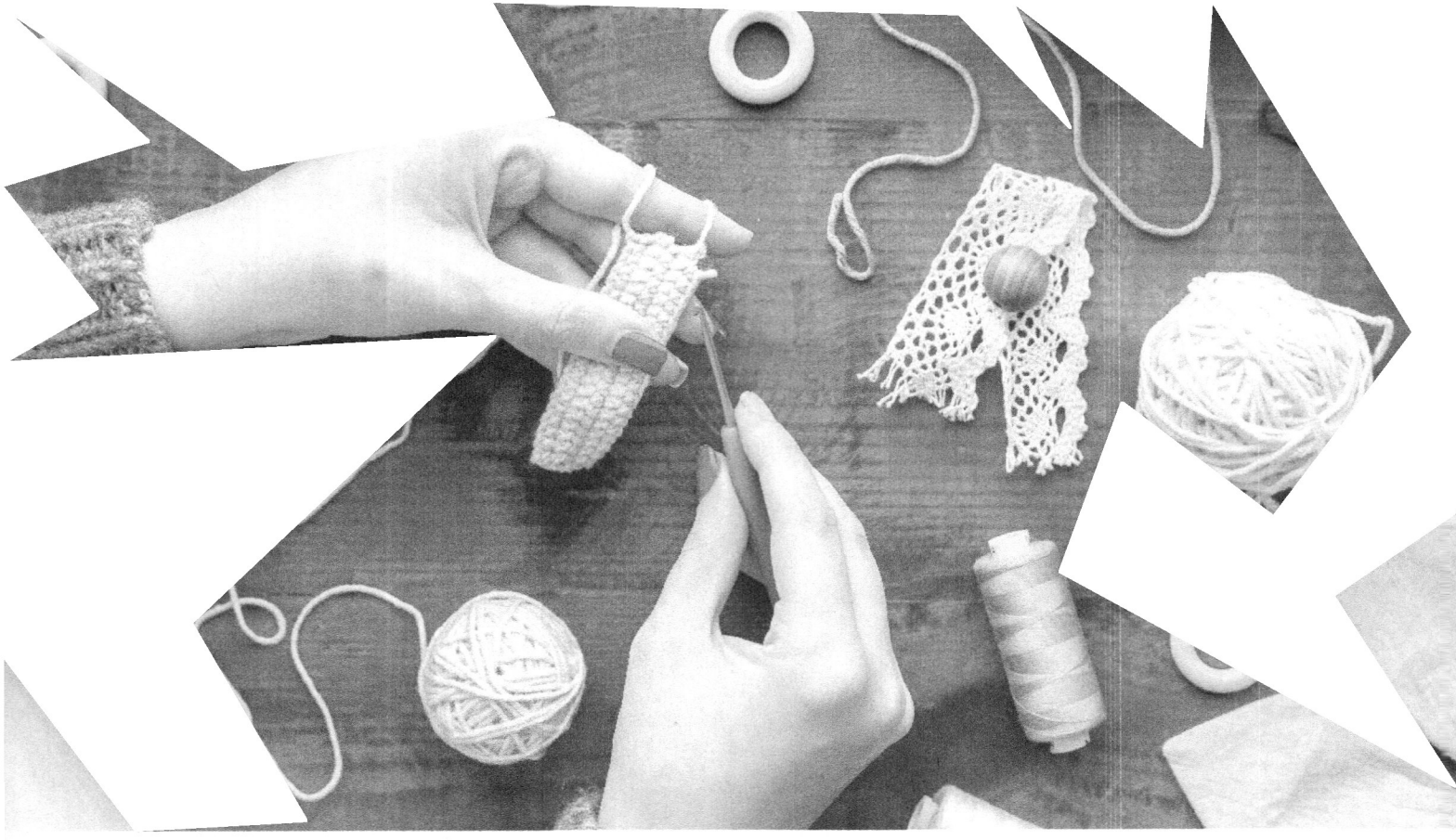

What Is Crochet?

Crochet is a craft that involves using a hook and yarn or other fiber to create fabric by looping yarn through a series of stitches. It is a type of needlework that is often used to create clothing, blankets, and other decorative items. In crochet, your crochet's hook is used to draw out yarn's loops through other loops to make a variety of different stitches. These stitches can be combined in various ways to create different textures, patterns, and shapes. Crochet can be done using a variety of different types of yarn. Each type of yarn can create a different texture or look, so choosing the right type of yarn is an important part of any crochet project. Crochet can be done by people of all ages and skill levels, from beginners to experienced crocheters. It's a great craft that can be used to create a wide range of items, from simple dishcloths to intricate lace shawls. With a practice and patience, anyone can learn to crochet and create beautiful handmade items.

History Of Crochet

The history of crochet is somewhat disputed, with different theories about its origins. However, most sources agree that crochet as we know it today likely developed in Europe in the early 19th century. One theory is that crochet may have evolved from a type of embroidery known as tambour work, which was popular in France in the 18th century. Tambour work involved using a hook to create loops of thread on a fabric surface, similar to the way crochet is worked. Another theory is that crochet may have developed from a type of lace-making called "nun's work." This technique used a small, hooked needle to create a chain stitch, which could then be worked into a lace pattern. Regardless of its origins, crochet became popular in Europe in the 19th century as a way to create lace and other decorative items. It was also used to make practical items such as clothing, blankets, and household items. Crochet spread to other parts of the world in the 20th century, becoming especially popular in the United States. Today, crochet is a beloved hobby practiced by individuals of all backgrounds, and continues to evolve with new techniques, patterns, and materials.

Difference Between Crochet And Weaving

Crochet and weaving are both textile arts, but they are quite different in the techniques used and the results produced. Crochet involves using a hook to create loops of yarn or other fiber, which are then pulled through other loops to create a variety of stitches. Crochet is a type of needlework that is done by hand, and it's often used to create clothing, blankets, and other decorative items. In crochet, each stitch is made individually, one at a time, and the fabric is built up row by row. Weaving, on the other hand, involves interlacing threads or other fibers over and under each other to create a fabric. Weaving can be done on a loom, which is a device that holds the threads in place while the weaver works, or it can be done by hand using a simple frame or other improvised device. Weaving is often used to create fabrics for clothing or household items, such as towels or rugs. In weaving, the threads are usually pre-wound onto a warp, and the weft is woven in and out of the warp strings to create the fabric.

Crochet for Beginners

Difference Between Crochet And Tatting

The main difference between crochet and tatting is in the techniques used to create the fabric. Crochet uses a hook to create loops that are then pulled through other loops, while tatting uses a shuttle or needle to create knots and loops that are combined in specific patterns. Additionally, the fabrics produced by each technique have different textures and densities. Crochet produces a thicker, more dense fabric, while tatting produces a delicate, lacy fabric. Overall, both crochet and tatting are beautiful and rewarding needlework techniques that offer unique opportunities for creativity and self-expression.

What Can You Make With Crochet

Crochet is a versatile art form that offers endless possibilities for creative expression. From intricate lace doilies and delicate shawls to chunky blankets and playful amigurumi toys, crochet can be used to create a range of things. In this essay, we will explore the versatility of crochet art and how it can be used to create a range of different projects. One of the most versatile aspects of crochet is the ability to use a wide range of yarns, colors, and textures. Crocheters can choose from natural fibers like wool, cotton, and silk or synthetic fibers like acrylic, nylon, and polyester. The thickness of the yarn can also be varied, from thin lace weight yarns to thick and chunky options. This range of materials allows crocheters to create anything from delicate lace items to sturdy home decor. Here are some of the great things that you can make using this art:

Blankets and Afghans: Crocheted blankets and Afghans are cozy and warm, and can be made in a variety of patterns and styles.

Hats and scarves: Crocheted hats and scarves are stylish and practical, and can be made in a variety of colors and textures.

Amigurumi: Amigurumi is a Japanese form of crocheting or knitting small, stuffed yarn creatures or dolls. The term "amigurumi" is derived from "Ami," (a Japanese word) which means knitted or crocheted, and "nuigurumi," means stuffed doll. Amigurumi typically involves crocheting small, detailed parts, such as limbs, ears, and tails, and then assembling them to create a cute, soft toy. The toys are often made using a small hook and fine yarn to create tight, neat stitches.

Clothing: Crochet can be used to create all sorts of clothing items, from shawls and wraps to tops and dresses.

Home decor: Crocheted items can add a cozy touch to your home decor. You can make things like doilies, pillow covers, and even crocheted baskets. rochet can be used to make all sorts of beautiful and unique home decor items. Here are some ideas:

- Doilies: Crocheted doilies can be used to decorate tables, shelves, and other surfaces.
- Pillow covers: Crochet pillow covers can add a cozy touch to your living room or bedroom.
- Wall hangings: Crochet wall hangings can add a touch of bohemian style to any room.
- Coasters: Crocheted coasters are a practical and stylish addition to any coffee table.
- Baskets: Crocheted baskets are a great way to store small items like keys, phone chargers, and other odds and ends.
- Rugs: Crocheted rugs can add a cozy touch to your floors.

Accessories: Crochet accessories can be a fun and stylish way to add some handmade touches to your wardrobe. Here are some ideas for crochet accessories:

- Hats: Crocheted hats can be made in different styles and colors to match your personal style. From slouchy beanies to cozy earflap hats, there are many hat patterns to choose from.
- Scarves and cowls: Crocheted scarves and cowls can add warmth and style to any outfit. You can make them in a variety of colors and patterns, and use different yarns to create interesting textures.
- Mittens and gloves: Crocheted mittens and gloves can be a great way to keep your hands warm in the winter. You can make them in a variety of colors and patterns, and use different yarns to create interesting textures.
- Bags and purses: Crocheted bags and purses can be a fun and unique way to carry your essentials. You can make them in a variety of sizes

and styles, and use different colors and yarns to create interesting patterns.
- Jewelry: Crocheted jewelry can be a fun and creative way to add some color and texture to your outfits. You can make earrings, necklaces, and bracelets using a variety of yarns and beads.
- Belts: Crocheted belts can be a fun and unique way to add some color and texture to your outfits. You can make them in a variety of colors and patterns, and use different yarns to create interesting textures.

Baby items: Crochet baby items can be a fun and rewarding way to create handmade gifts for little ones. Here are some ideas for crochet baby items:

- Baby blankets: Crocheted baby blankets are a classic gift that can be kept for years to come. You can make them in a variety of sizes and colors, and use different yarns to create interesting textures.
- Booties: Crocheted baby booties can be a fun and stylish way to keep little feet warm. You can make them in a variety of colors and patterns, and use different yarns to create interesting textures.
- Sweaters and cardigans: Crocheted baby sweaters and cardigans can be a fun way to keep little ones warm. You can make them in a variety of colors and patterns, and use different yarns to create interesting textures.
- Toys: Crocheted baby toys can be a fun and creative way to stimulate a baby's senses. You can make rattles, stuffed animals, and other toys using a variety of yarns and colors.
- Pacifier clips: Crocheted pacifier clips can be a fun and practical way to keep a baby's pacifier within reach. You can make them in a variety of colors and patterns, and use different yarns to create interesting textures.

Chapter 2:
Choosing The Perfect Crocheting Supplies

Crochet tools are essential for any crocheter to produce beautiful and intricate designs. From the essential crochet hook and yarn to the optional tools like stitch markers, yarn bowls, and ergonomic hooks, each tool has a specific function that contributes to the success of the project. Whether you are a newbie or a well-experienced crocheter, having the right tools can make crocheting more enjoyable and rewarding. Crochet tools can be found in a variety of places, both online and in physical stores. Many craft stores carry a wide selection of crochet tools, including crochet hooks, yarn, stitch markers, and more. Some popular craft store chains include Michaels, Joann, and Hobby Lobby.

There are many online shops that are selling crochet tools and supplies. Some popular options include Amazon, Etsy, and LoveCrafts. Yarn shops often carry a range of crochet tools, including crochet hooks, stitch markers, and yarn. They may also offer classes and workshops to help you learn new techniques. Some local markets may have vendors who sell handmade crochet items and tools. This can be a great way to support local artisans and find unique crochet tools and supplies. 2ndhand stores like Goodwill and Salvation Army can sometimes have crochet hooks and other tools at a much lower cost. It's important to inspect 2ndhand tools carefully to ensure that they are still in good condition.

When shopping for crochet tools, it's important to consider the quality of the tools as well as the price. High-quality tools may cost more upfront, but they will last longer and make crocheting more enjoyable in the long run. It's also a good idea to read their reviews and do some research before purchasing crochet tools to know for sure that you are getting the best product for your needs. Following is a list of all the crochet tools, essentials or supplies that you will need to get started with your crochet projects:

Crochet hooks:

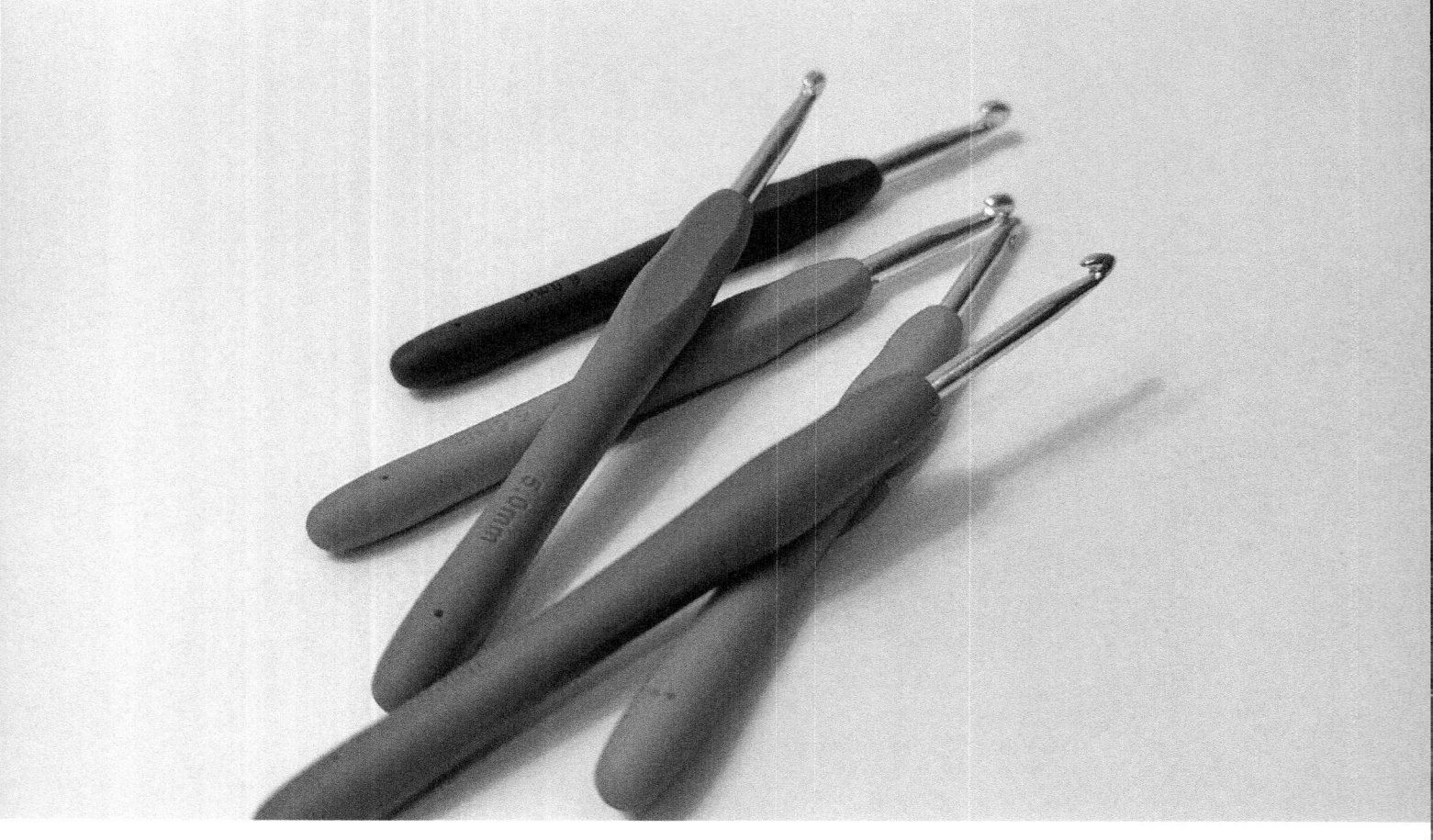

These are the most important tools you will need for crocheting. Choose a set of hooks in different sizes to accommodate different yarn weights. Crochet hooks are the primary tool used in crocheting. They are slender, tapered tools that are designed to pull out yarn's loops through other loops to create crochet stitches. Crochet hooks are typically made of materials such as plastic, steel, aluminum, or bamboo, and come in varying sizes ranging from small (such as a US steel hook size 14) to large (such as a US hook size Q or 16 mm). The size of your crochet's hook you choose will depend on the thickness and texture of the yarn you are using, as well as the stitch pattern and tension you want to achieve. Crochet hooks have a pointed end and a smooth, curved hook that is used to catch and pull out the yarn through loops. Some crochet hooks also have ergonomic handles or grips, which can help to reduce hand fatigue and make crocheting more comfortable for those with arthritis or other hand conditions.

Types of Hooks

Crochet hooks can be purchased individually or in sets, and it's a good idea to have a range of sizes on hand to accommodate different yarns and projects. When selecting a hook, be sure to check the suggested hook size on the yarn label or in the pattern you are using to ensure you are using the correct size. There are many types of crochet hooks, each with its own unique features and benefits. Here are some types of crochet hooks:

Aluminum hooks: These are the most common type of crochet hooks and are lightweight, durable, and affordable.

Steel hooks: These are smaller hooks that are used for crocheting with fine, laceweight yarns. They are often used for making doilies and other delicate projects.

Plastic hooks: These are lightweight, comfortable to hold, and often come in bright colors. They are a good choice for beginners, as they are affordable and easy to work with.

Bamboo hooks: These are eco-friendly, lightweight, and have a warm feel in the hand. They are good for working with slippery or sensitive fibers, as they have a slightly textured surface that helps to grip the yarn.

Tunisian crochet hooks: These are longer than regular crochet hooks and have a plastic stopper at the end. They are used for Tunisian crochet, also known as Afghan crochet, which creates a fabric that looks like a mix between knitting and crochet.

Double-ended crochet hooks: These are hooks that have a hook on both ends, which allows you to work in the round without turning your work.

Interchangeable crochet hooks: These are sets of hooks that allow you to switch out different sizes and styles of hooks without having to purchase a new set. They are convenient for those who crochet frequently or like to have many hook sizes on hand.

There are also many other types of crochet hooks available, including ergonomic hooks, light-up hooks, and hooks with built-in counters or stitch markers. Choosing the right type of hook will depend on your personal preference, the type of project you are working on, and the yarn you are using.

Crochet Hook Sizes

They come in a variety of sizes, which are usually measured in millimeters (mm) or letter/number sizes (such as "G" or "H"). The size of your crochet's hook you use will depend on the yarn's weight you're using, as well as the desired outcome of your project. Here are some common sizes of crochet hooks:

B-1 Crochet Hook: It has the thickness of 2.25 mm

C-2 Crochet Hook: It has the thickness of 2.75 mm

D-3 Crochet Hook: It has the thickness of 3.25 mm

E-4 Crochet Hook: It has the thickness of 3.5 mm

F-5 Crochet Hook: It has the thickness of 3.75 mm

G-6 Crochet Hook: It has the thickness of 4.0 mm

H-8 Crochet Hook: It has the thickness of 5.0 mm

I-9 Crochet Hook: It has the thickness of 5.5 mm

J-10 Crochet Hook: It has the thickness of 6.0 mm

K-10.5 Crochet Hook: It has the thickness of 6.5 mm

L-11 Crochet Hook: It has the thickness of 8.0 mm

M-13 Crochet Hook: It has the thickness of 9.0 mm

N-15 Crochet Hook: It has the thickness of 10.0 mm

P-16 Crochet Hook: It has the thickness of 11.5 mm

Q Crochet Hook: It has the thickness of 16.0 mm

These sizes are not universal and can vary slightly depending on the brand and country of origin. It's always a great idea to check the label of your yarn to see what size hook is recommended, and to test out different hook sizes until you find the one that works best for your project.

Yarn

Choose a yarn that is appropriate for your project. Look for yarns that are labeled with the recommended hook size, weight, and fiber content. Crochet yarn is a type of yarn that is specifically designed for use in crochet projects. It is typically created from a variety of different materials, including wool, cotton, acrylic, and even bamboo, among others. The weight or thickness of the yarn is often indicated on the label using a number system, which ranges from super fine to super bulky. The weight of the yarn can determine how quickly a project will work up and how it will look. Different types of crochet projects may require different types of yarn. For example, a delicate lace shawl may require a thinner yarn, while a warm and cozy blanket may require a bulkier yarn. It is important to choose the appropriate yarn weight for your project to ensure the finished product turns out the way you intended.

Types of Yarn (By Material)

Crochet yarn comes in a variety of types, each with its unique characteristics. Here are some common types of crochet yarn:

Acrylic Yarn: This yarn is a synthetic material made from polymer fibers. It is affordable, durable, and comes in a variety of colors.

Wool Yarn: This type of yarn is made from animal fibers, usually from sheep. Wool yarn is warm, breathable, and often used for winter garments and accessories.

Cotton Yarn: This type of yarn is made from natural cotton fibers. It is soft, breathable, and often used for summer garments and dishcloths.

Bamboo Yarn: This type of yarn is made from bamboo fibers. It is soft, lightweight, and often used for baby garments and accessories.

Silk Yarn: This type of yarn is made from silk fibers. It is luxurious, smooth, and often used for elegant garments and accessories.

Alpaca Yarn: This type of yarn is made from the fleece of alpacas. It is soft, warm, and often used for winter garments and accessories.

Mohair Yarn: This type of yarn is created from the hair of the Angora goat. It is soft, fluffy, and often used for fuzzy accessories like scarves and hats.

Chenille Yarn: This type of yarn is made from velvety yarn piles that resemble caterpillars. It is soft, plush, and often used for baby garments and blankets.

There are many other types of crochet yarn available, but these are some of the most common.

Yarns By Thickness

In crochet, yarn thickness or weight refers to the thickness or diameter of the yarn. There are several different weight categories of yarn, and each weight is designated by a number or name. The weight of the yarn is an important factor to consider when selecting a yarn for a crochet project, as it can affect the texture, drape, and overall appearance of the finished item. Here are the most common yarn weight categories, listed from the thinnest to the thickest:

Lace weight: This is the thinnest yarn weight category, and it is often used for delicate, lacy crochet projects. Lace weight yarns have a diameter of 0 to 1.7 mm.

Fingering weight: This yarn weight is slightly thicker than lace weight, with a diameter of 1.8 to 2.75 mm. Fingering weight yarns are often used for socks, shawls, and other lightweight projects.

Sport weight: Sport weight yarn has a diameter of 2.75 to 3.5 mm, and it is often used for lightweight sweaters, scarves, and baby items.

Worsted weight: This is the most commonly used yarn weight, with a diameter of 3.5 to 4.5 mm. Worsted weight yarns are versatile and can be used for a wide range of projects, from hats and scarves to blankets and sweaters.

Bulky weight: Bulky weight yarns have a diameter of 5 to 6 mm, and they are often used for warm, cozy projects like hats, scarves, and blankets.

Super bulky weight: This is the thickest yarn weight category, with a diameter of 6.5 mm or larger. Super bulky weight yarns are great for quick and easy projects, like blankets and scarves.

When selecting a yarn for a crochet project, it's important to consider the weight of the yarn, as well as the recommended hook size for that yarn. Using the wrong weight of yarn or hook size can result in a project that is too loose or too tight, and may not look or feel the way you want it to.

Yarn needle:

This is a large-eyed needle that is used for weaving in ends and connecting pieces together. A yarn needle, also known as a tapestry needle or a darning needle, is a large needle used for sewing knitted or crocheted pieces together or weaving in ends of yarn to finish a project. Yarn needles typically have a large eye to accommodate the thickness of yarn and a blunt tip to prevent splitting the yarn fibers. They are also usually longer than regular sewing needles to make it easier to weave in ends or sew pieces together. Yarn needles come in a variety of materials such as plastic, metal, and wood, and can be found in different sizes. They are an essential tool for finishing any knitting or crochet project and can be used to sew together seams, attach buttons, and weave in loose ends to create a neat and finished look.

Stitch markers:

They are small tools used by knitters and crocheters to mark a specific stitch or location in their work. They can be made of plastic, metal, or a variety of other materials and come in a range of sizes and shapes. Stitch markers are used for a variety of purposes. They can help you keep track of where you are in a pattern, mark the beginning of a round or row, indicate a specific stitch that needs attention, or mark the placement of an increase or decrease. Stitch markers can be removable or fixed. Removable stitch markers can be easily added and removed from your work, allowing you to reuse them in different parts of your project. Fixed stitch markers are usually placed on the needle and cannot be removed until you come to them in your work. There are a variety of stitch markers available to suit different knitting and crochet projects, including locking stitch markers, split-ring stitch markers, and coil less safety pins. Choosing the right stitch marker for your project can help make your work easier and more enjoyable.

Other Tools

Measuring tape: This is essential for checking gauge and measuring your finished project.

Crochet Directions: Choose a pattern that is appropriate for your skill level and the project you want to make.

Stitch dictionary: This is a reference book that contains Directions for different crochet stitches.

Blocking tools: These can include a blocking mat, blocking pins, and spray bottle to shape and smooth your finished project. Blocking is an important process for finishing a crochet project, and there are a variety of tools that can be used to help with this process. Here are some common blocking tools for crochet:

Blocking Mats: These are foam mats that are used to block your crochet project. They are often covered with a grid to help you measure and space your project.

T-Pins: These are long, thin pins with a T-shaped head. They are used to hold your crochet project in place on the blocking mat.

Blocking Wires: These are thin, flexible wires that can be threaded through the edges of your crochet project to help shape and stretch it during blocking.

Spray Bottle: This can be used to dampen your crochet project before blocking, which can help it hold its shape.

Steam Iron: This can be used to steam your crochet project, which can help it hold its shape and smooth out any wrinkles.

Measuring Tape: This can be used to measure your crochet project and ensure that it is blocked to the correct dimensions.

Clothesline and Clothespins: These can be used to create a hanging system for blocking items like shawls or scarves.

Using these tools, you can block your crochet project to the correct shape and size, which can help it look more polished and professional.

Crochet project bag: A bag to store your supplies and works-in-progress is helpful to keep everything organized.

These are the basic supplies needed to start crocheting. As you progress in your skills and interests, you may want to add more specialized tools and materials to your collection.

Chapter 3:
How To Understand and Read Crochet Patterns

Reading a pattern of a crochet project may looks intimidating at 1st, but once you understand the basics, it can be a very helpful tool for creating a wide range of crochet projects. The 1st thing you should need to do when reading a crochet pattern is to understand the pattern key. This will tell you what all the abbreviations and symbols mean in the pattern. A pattern key, also known as a stitch glossary, include abbreviations and symbols which are used in a crochet pattern, along with their corresponding full names or descriptions. The key is usually included at the beginning of the pattern and is an essential part of understanding and following the pattern correctly. Here are some common abbreviations you might find in a pattern key for crochet:

Crochet Stitch	**Abbreviations**
Chain	Ch
Double crochet	Dc
Decrease -Remove 1 or more stitches	Dec
Half double crochet	Hdc
Increase - Add 1 or more stitches	Inc
Repeat	Rep
Single crochet	Sc
Slip stitch	Sl st
Skip	Sk
Stitches	St(s)
Treble crochet	Tr

A pattern key may also include symbols that indicate specific Directions or stitches. For example, a **dot** (.) might be used to indicate a slip stitch (st), or an asterisk (*) might be used to indicate a repeated section of the pattern. It's important to read the pattern key carefully before beginning any crochet project to ensure that you understand all the abbreviations and symbols used in the pattern. This will make it easier to follow the pattern and create a finished project that looks just like the one in the pattern. Read the entire pattern from start to finish to get an idea of what the project involves. Pay attention to the required materials, gauge, and any special Directions.

Gauge

It is the "number of stitches and rows per inch", and it's important to check that your gauge matches the gauge given in the pattern. This will ensure that your finished project is the correct size. It is an important aspect of following a crochet pattern and creating a finished project that matches the size and shape of the pattern. Every crochet pattern will specify a gauge, and it's important to check your gauge before beginning the project to ensure that your finished item will be the correct size. To check your gauge, you can crochet a swatch, usually a 4x4 inch (10x10 cm) square, using the specified hook size and yarn. You can then count the number of stitches and rows in the square to see if they match the gauge given in the pattern.

If your gauge is different from the pattern gauge, you may need to adjust your hook size or yarn weight to achieve the correct gauge. For example, if your swatch has fewer stitches per inch than the pattern gauge, you may need to use a smaller-sized hook to gain the correct tension. If your swatch has more stitches per inch than the pattern gauge, you may need to use a larger hook size. Getting gauge right is especially important for projects where the size matters, such as clothing or items that need to fit together with other pieces. Checking and adjusting gauge can ensure that your finished project is the right size and shape, and will look the way it was intended to by the designer.

Once you understand the abbreviations and gauge, follow the pattern step by step. Each row or round will be clearly marked, and you should work through them one at a time. As you work through the pattern, check your work mostly to make sure that you haven't made any mistakes. Once you have completed all the steps in the pattern, finish the project according to the pattern Directions. This may involve weaving in ends, adding embellishments, or blocking the project.

Chapter 4:
Different Basic Stitches Of Crochet

Crochet stitches are the building blocks of any crochet project, from simple scarves and hats to intricate lacework and Afghans. There are countless crochet stitches to choose from, each with its own unique look and texture. In this chapter, we'll explore some of the most popular and useful crochet stitches and their various applications. Here are some of the commonly used basic crochet stitches:

Slip Stitch or Slipknot

A slipknot is a basic knot used in crochet and other crafts that involves making a loop with one end of the yarn and passing the other end through the loop to create a knot. It is the 1st step in starting many crochet projects and is also used to connect a new ball of yarn to an existing project. To make a slipknot, follow these steps:

- Take the end of your yarn and create a small loop by wrapping the yarn around your fingers.
- Bring the end of your crochet yarn that is coming from the ball over the loop then push it underneath the loop.
- Hold the point where the two ends of the yarn meet with your fingers and pull out this end of your yarn through the crochet loop.
- Adjust the loop size and tension by pulling on the two ends of the yarn until you have the desired size.

Once you have made the slipknot, you can push your crochet hook through the loop and begin your 1st crochet stitch.

Ch-Chain Stitch :

This is the most basic stitch in crochet. It is used to create the foundation chain, as well as to add stitches to a row. To make this stitch, move over the yarn then pull out your yarn through the loop on the crochet's hook. It is one of the most fundamental stitches in crochet. It is typically used as the foundation for many other stitches and is also used to create openwork and lacy designs.

- Make a slipknot on your hook.
- Wrap over your crochet yarn on your hook from back-side to the front.
- With the crochet hook in your hand, pull out the wrapped yarn through the slipknot, forming a new loop on the crochet's hook. This will be your 1st chain stitch.
- Continue by repeating those steps 2 and 3 to make additional chain stitches.

To create a longer chain, simply Continue by repeating those steps 2 and 3 as many times as necessary. To practice your chain stitch, you can create a chain of any length, and then undo it and Continue by repeating the process until you feel comfortable with the stitch. The chain stitch is also commonly used in combination with other stitches to create a wide variety of crochet projects.

Single crochet:

This stitch is used to create a dense fabric with little to no gaps between stitches. To make a single crochet, push your crochet's hook into that stitch, move over the yarn, and pull out this hook through a loop. Pass your over yarn again and draw it through both those loops on the crochet's hook. Here's how you can make it:

- Push your crochet's hook into the 2nd chain from your hook (without considering the hook's loop). That's where you will start your 1st single crochet stitch.
- Wrap over this yarn on your crochet's hook from the back-side to the front.
- Pull out the wrapped yarn through the chain stitch, so that there are 2 loops created on the crochet's hook.
- Wrap over this yarn on your crochet's hook again from the back-side to the front.
- Pull out the wrapped yarn through the loops. This completes one single crochet stitch.

To make additional single crochet stitches, simply continue by repeating those steps 1 through 5, pushing your hook into the adjacent crochet chain stitch and working through those 2 loops created on the crochet's hook until you reach the row's end.

The single crochet stitch creates a dense, tight fabric, and is often used for amigurumi, dishcloths, and other projects that require a sturdy, durable fabric.

Half Double crochet:

It creates a fabric with some texture and drape. To make this stitch, pass over the yarn, push the crochet hook into the stitch, pass over the yarn, and create a loop. Pass over the yarn again pull out then through all three loops on the crochet's hook.

- Pass over the yarn your crochet's hook from the back-side to the front.
- Push your crochet's hook into the 3rd chain from your crochet's hook (without considering the hook's loop). This is where you will start your 1st half double crochet stitch.
- Pass over your yarn on your crochet's hook again from the back-side to the front.
- Pull out the wrapped yarn through the chain stitch, so that there are three loops on the crochet's hook.
- Pass over the yarn on your crochet's hook again from the back-side to the front.
- Pull out the wrapped yarn through all 3 loops. This completes one half double crochet stitch.

To make additional half double crochet stitches, simply continue by repeating those steps 2 through 6, pushing your hook into the adjacent crochet chain stitch and working through the three loops on the crochet's hook until you reach the row's end. The half double crochet stitch creates a fabric that is taller and looser than the single crochet stitch, and is often used for scarves, hats, and other projects that require a bit more drape and flexibility than the single crochet stitch.

Double crochet:

This stitch is comparatively taller than the half double crochet, and creates a looser fabric with more drape. To make this stitch, pass over the yarn the hook,, push your hook into the stitch, again pass over the yarn on the hook, and create a loop. Pass over the yarn on the hook again and draw it through those 2 loops on your crochet's hook, then move pass over your yarn on the hook then draw through the remaining two crochet loops.

- Bring the yarn from the back-side to the front your crochet's hook
- Push your crochet hook into that 4th chain from this hook(without considering the hook's loop). This is where you will start your 1st double crochet stitch.
- Again, bring yarn from the back-side to the front your crochet's hook.
- Pull out the wrapped yarn through the chain stitch, so that there are 3 loops on the crochet's hook.
- Again, bring yarn from the back-side to the front your crochet's hook.
- Pull out the wrapped yarn through the 1st two loops created on the crochet's hook, so that there are 2 loops remaining on the crochet's hook.
- Again, bring yarn from the back-side to the front your crochet's hook.
- Draw out the wrapped yarn through those last 2 loops. This completes 1 double crochet stitch.

To make additional double crochet stitches, simply continue by repeating those steps 2 through 8, pushing your hook into the adjacent crochet chain stitch and working through those 2 loops created on the crochet's hook until you reach the row's end. The double crochet stitch creates a fabric that is open and airy, and is often used for blankets, shawls, and other projects that require a lightweight and breathable fabric. It can also be combined with other stitches, such as the chain stitch and the half double crochet stitch, to create a wide variety of crochet projects.

Treble Crochet :

This stitch is comparatively taller than the double crochet and creates a very loose fabric with a lot of drape. It is also known as the triple crochet stitch in some countries. To make a treble crochet stitch, follow these steps:

- Begin by making a foundation chain of the desired length. Then, pass over the yarn twice.
- Push your crochet's hook into that 4th chain from your hook (that's the 1st stitch you will be working into).
- Pass over the yarn then draw a loop. You will now have four loops on this hook.
- Pass the thread over then draw through the 1st two loops. You will now have three loops on your crochet's hook.
- Pass over the yarn then draw through the adjacent 2 loops. There will now be 2 loops.
- Pass over the yarn then draw through the last 2 loops. You will now have completed one treble crochet stitch.
- To make the adjacent treble crochet stitch, pass over this yarn on your crochet's hook twice again and push your crochet's hook into the adjacent stitch. Continue by repeating those steps 3 to 6 until you have completed the desired number of stitches.
- The treble crochet stitch creates a very open and lacy fabric and is often used in projects like shawls, Afghans, and other large items.

These are just a few of the basic crochet stitches that you can use to create a wide variety of projects. By combining different stitches and playing with colors and textures, you can create unique and beautiful crochet items.

Chapter 5:
Crochet For Right And Left Handers

The main difference between left and right hand crocheters is the direction in which they hold their crochet hooks and yarn. For example, right hand crocheters typically work in a clockwise direction, while left hand crocheters work in a counterclockwise direction. This means that when following a pattern, left hand crocheters may need to reverse the Directions in order to achieve the same result.

In addition to the basic differences in how your crochet's hook and yarn are held, left and right hand crocheters may also find that they have differences in tension and stitch formation. Left hand crocheters may need to adjust their tension in order to achieve the same gauge as a right hand crocheter, and may also find that some stitches come out differently due to the opposite direction in which your crochet's hook is turned. Despite these differences, left and right hand crocheters can both achieve beautiful and intricate crochet work. Many patterns and tutorials are available for both left and right hand crocheters, and with practice and patience, anyone can become skilled at this enjoyable craft. Here are some tips for both right and left-handed crocheters to help you get started:

For Right-Handed Crocheters:

- Hold the yarn in your left-hand while holding the hook in the right.
- Make sure the crochet yarn is wrapped around your left hand for tension control.
- Use your right hand to hold your crochet's hook and manipulate the yarn to create stitches.

Most crochet patterns are written for right-handed crocheters, so make sure to read the pattern carefully before you start.

For Left-Handed Crocheters:

- Hold the yarn in your right-hand while holding the hook in the left.
- Make sure the yarn is wrapped around your right hand for tension control.

- Use your left hand to hold your crochet's hook and manipulate the yarn to create stitches.
- Some crochet patterns may need to be adapted for left-handed crocheters, such as reversing the order of stitches or turning the pattern upside down.

Chapter 6:
How To Avoid Most Common Mistakes

Crochet is a fun and creative hobby, but it can also be frustrating when mistakes are made. Even the most experienced crocheters make mistakes, but identifying and correcting these mistakes can help prevent them from happening in the future. In this chapter, we'll explore some common crochet mistakes and how to fix them.

Tight stitches

Tight stitches are a common mistake that many beginners make when learning to crochet. Tight stitches can make it difficult to work into the stitches and cause the finished piece to be stiff and inflexible. Here is how to avoid it:

- **Relax your grip**: One of the main causes of tight stitches is gripping the yarn and hook too tightly. Try to relax your grip and hold the yarn and hook loosely.
- **Use a larger hook**: Using a larger hook can help to create looser stitches. If you find that your stitches are too tight, try using a hook that is one or two sizes bigger than the recommended size for the yarn.
- **Practice with scrap yarn**: Practice making a few rows of stitches with scrap yarn before starting your project. This can help you get a feel for the tension and ensure that your stitches are not too tight.
- **Check your tension**: As you work, check your tension frequently by laying your work flat and ensuring that the stitches are not too tightly packed together.
- **Block your work**: After completing your project, blocking can help to relax the stitches and create a more even and flexible fabric.

Remember that it takes practice and patience to develop good crochet habits, and it's okay to make mistakes. By focusing on keeping a relaxed grip and practicing with a variety of yarn and hook sizes, you can improve your crochet skills and create beautiful pieces.

Uneven Tension

Uneven tension is another common crochet mistake that beginners may encounter. Uneven tension can result in lumpy or uneven stitches, making the finished piece look distorted or unprofessional. Here is how to avoid uneven tension in your crochet work:

- **Practice maintaining a consistent tension**: One of the most crucial things you can do to achieve even tension is to practice maintaining a consistent tension as you crochet. Try to keep the yarn taut but not too tight, and aim to make your stitches all the same size.
- **Use the right hook size**: Your crochet's hook size you use can also impact your tension. If your stitches are too tight or too loose, try switching to a smaller or larger hook size, respectively.
- **Take breaks**: It's important to take breaks as you work to avoid fatigue, which can cause uneven tension. Stretch your hands and arms, and take a break if you start to feel any pain or discomfort.
- **Keep your yarn organized**: Keeping your yarn organized and untangled can also help you maintain even tension. Use a yarn bowl or bag to keep your yarn contained, and make sure it's not getting tangled or twisted as you work.

Losing Track Of Stitches

Losing track of stitches is a common mistake that many beginners make when learning to crochet. It's easy to get confused or lose count of the stitches, especially in the beginning when the work looks similar on both sides. Here is how to avoid losing track of stitches:

- **Use stitch markers**: Using stitch markers can help you keep track of your stitches and make it easier to count them. You can use a different color or type of stitch marker to dot the starting of each round or row.

- **Count your stitches frequently:** Make a habit of counting your stitches after every few rows or rounds to ensure that you haven't missed any. This will also help you catch any mistakes early on.
- **Learn how to check the different types of stitches:** Learning to identify the different types of stitches can help you count your stitches more accurately. Make sure you can identify the chain stitch- Ch, single crochet, and any other stitches used in the pattern.
- **Don't rush:** Crocheting is a relaxing and meditative activity, and it's important to take your time and work slowly and carefully. Rushing can cause mistakes and make it harder to keep track of your stitches.
- **Use a row counter:** If you're working on a larger project, it may be helpful to use a row counter to track the number of rows or rounds you've completed.

Not Reading The Pattern Carefully

Not reading the pattern carefully is another common mistake that many crocheters make, especially beginners. When you don't read the pattern carefully, you can miss important details, skip stitches, or misunderstand the Directions.

- **Read the entire pattern before you begin:** Take the time to read the entire pattern before you begin. This will give you a right idea of the project and help you avoid any surprises or unexpected difficulties.
- **Use a highlighter or sticky notes:** Use a highlighter or sticky notes to mark important sections or Directions in the pattern.
- **Pay attention to the details:** Take the time to read each instruction carefully and pay attention to the details. Check for any special stitches or abbreviations, and make sure you understand what each instruction is asking you to do.
- **Double-check your work:** After completing each step or row, double-check your work to make sure you've followed the Directions

correctly. This will help you catch any mistakes early on and avoid having to rip out your work later.

By reading the pattern carefully and paying attention to the details, you can avoid mistakes and create beautiful crochet projects

Forgetting To Turn Your Work:

Forgetting to turn your work is a common mistake that many beginners make in crochet. This mistake can cause your work to become twisted or lopsided, and it can be frustrating to undo your work and start over. Here are some tips to turn your work:

- **Make use of a stitch marker**: To keep track of the direction you're working in, use a stitch marker to indicate each row's end. Once you reach the end of a row, shift the stitch marker to the 1st stitch of the adjacent row. This technique will assist you in maintaining a sense of direction as you work.
- **Say it out loud:** Saying 'turn" out loud at each row's end can help you remember to turn your work. This can also help you stay focused and avoid making other mistakes.
- **Make a mental note**: Before you start working on the adjacent row, make a mental note to turn your work. This will help you remember to do it, even if you get distracted or lose track of what you're doing.
- **Use a pattern with clear Directions:** Using a pattern with clear Directions can also help you remember to turn your work. Look for patterns that include the instruction "turn" at each row's end.

Wrong Yarn Weight Or Hook Size:

Using the wrong yarn weight or hook size is a common mistake that can affect the finished size and appearance of your crochet project.

- **Check the yarn label**: Check the label on the yarn for information about the recommended hook size and gauge. This will help you choose the right hook size and ensure that your finished project is the right size and shape.
- **Use a yarn weight chart**: Use a yarn weight chart to help you choose the right yarn weight for your project. Yarn weight is classified by a number system, and different weights require different hook sizes.
- **Make a gauge swatch**: To make sure that your finished project is the correct size, it's recommended to create a small gauge swatch using the yarn and hook size you intend to use before commencing your project. This enables you to verify that your tension is appropriate.
- **Consider the drape of the finished item**: The yarn weight and hook size you choose will affect the drape of the finished item. A larger hook size will create a more open, lacy fabric, while a smaller hook size will create a tighter, more dense fabric.
- **Be willing to adjust**: If your project isn't meeting your expectations, feel free to modify your yarn weight or hook size. You may need to increase or decrease the size to obtain the correct tension and attain the intended finished size.

Cutting Your Yarn Too Short:

Cutting your yarn too short can result in an unfinished or uneven edge. Make sure to leave a long tail to weave in at the end. Cutting your yarn too short in crochet can be a frustrating mistake, as it can leave you without enough yarn to finish your project. Here is how to avoid cutting your yarn too short:

- **Estimate how much yarn you will need**: Before you start your project, estimate how much yarn you will need to complete it. This will let you avoid running out of yarn before you finish.

- **Leave a long tail when starting**: When starting a new project, leave a long tail of yarn (about 6 inches or more) to weave in later. This will ensure that you have enough yarn to finish your project.
- **Don't cut your yarn until you're sure you're finished**: Avoid cutting your yarn until you're absolutely sure you're finished with it. If you're not sure, leave a long tail and continue working.
- **Use yarn connect techniques:** When you run out of yarn, use a yarn connect technique to add a new ball of yarn.
- **Keep extra yarn on hand**: If you're not sure how much yarn you will need, it's always a good idea to keep extra yarn on hand. This will ensure that you have enough yarn to finish your project, even if you make a mistake.

Remember that mistakes are a normal part of learning, and with practice and patience, you can improve your crochet skills and create beautiful pieces.

Chapter 7:
Best Tips And Tricks For Newbies

If you're new to crochet, it's important to start with the basics and work your way up to more advanced techniques. Here are some tips to get started with crochet:

Choose the right yarn and hook: When you're starting out, it's best to choose a smooth, medium-weight yarn in a light color, and a hook that is easy to handle.

Start with simple patterns: Start with simple patterns that use basic stitches. As you gain experience, you can move on to more complex patterns.

Practice good tension: Make sure to practice good tension in your stitches, as this will help ensure that your crochet project looks neat and even. If your stitches are too tight, try using a larger hook, and if they're too loose, try using a smaller hook.

Use stitch markers: Use stitch markers to help you keep track of your stitches, especially if you're working in the round. This will help you avoid mistakes and keep your work looking neat and even.

Take breaks: Crocheting can be repetitive and hard on your hands, so it's important to take breaks and relax your hands and wrists to prevent injury.

Learn from mistakes: Everyone makes mistakes when they're learning to crochet, so don't be discouraged if you make a mistake.

Connect to a crochet community: Connecting a crochet community, either online or in person, can be a great way to get inspiration, ask questions, and connect with other people who love to crochet.

Chapter 9:
Best Crochet Pattern Ideas And Projects

Crochet projects can be made at home using just a few basic tools, such as a crochet hook, yarn or thread, and a pattern. There are many different types of crochet projects that you can make, including blankets, scarves, hats, shawls, socks, and more. To get started, you'll need to choose a pattern for the project you want to make. Once you have a pattern, you can choose the type of yarn or thread that you want to use, as well as the appropriate size crochet hook for that yarn. Once you have your tools and materials, you can begin working on your project. It's important to follow the Directions in the pattern carefully, especially if you are new to crochet. Take your time and work at a pace that is comfortable for you. Crochet projects can be a great way to relax and unwind, and they also make wonderful gifts for family and friends.

Crochet Sweater Pattern

Supplies:

- Pick (any color of choice) a suitable yarn (worsted weight).
- Take a H/5mm sized crochet hook
- Scissors

- Yarn needle

Directions:

Back panel:

1. Chain 50.
2. Put your crochet hook in the 3rd chain from the top and make a double crochet. Repeat this over the remaining chains (48 dc).
3. Chain 2, turn, and double crochet on each stitch as you go (48 dc).
4. Repeat step 3 as necessary until the item measures 16 inches from the start..

Left panel:

5. Chain 20.
6. With your crochet hook, make a double crochet stitch in the 3rd chain. Then, continue in this manner for each subsequent chain until the row is complete (18 dc).
7. Chain 2, turn, and double crochet on each stitch as you go (18 dc).
8. Replicate step 3 up until the item measures 8 inches from the start..

Right panel:

9. Chain 20.
10. With your crochet hook, make a double crochet stitch in the 3rd chain. Then, continue in this manner for each subsequent chain until the row is complete (18 dc).
11. Chain 2, turn, and double crochet on each stitch as you go (18 dc).
12. Repeat step 3 as necessary until the item is 8 inches from the start.

Connecting panels:

13. Lay the back panel flat with the wrong side facing up.
14. Place the left panel on the side (left) of the back panel, with the side (right) facing up. Align the top and bottom edges of the panels.

15. Using a needle and yarn, sew the left panel to the back panel along the top and bottom edges.
16. Continue by repeating step 2 with the right panel on the right side of the back panel.
17. Weave in all ends.

Sleeves:

18. Attach the yarn to the bottom of the armhole.
19. Make a chain of 2. Perform a double crochet on each of the stitch around the armhole, working 2 double crochet stitches in the corner stitches.
20. Connect this chain using a slip stitch (st) to the 1st stitch of double crochet.
21. Make a chain of 2. Perform a double crochet on each of the stitch around the armhole, working 2 double crochet stitches in the corner stitches.
22. Connect this chain using a slip stitch (st) to the 1st stitch of double crochet.
23. Continue by repeating those steps 1-5 for the 2nd sleeve.

Finishing:

24. Weave in all ends.
25. Attach a button or zipper to the front of the sweater, if desired.

This is a basic pattern, so feel free to customize it by adding different stitch patterns, stripes, or other embellishments. Enjoy your new crochet sweater!

Lorena Jackson

Crocheted Hand Mittens

Supplies:

- Pick (in a color of choice) a suitable yarn (worsted weight).
- Take a G/4mm sized crochet hook
- Scissors
- Yarn needle

Crochet for Beginners

Directions:

1. Make a foundation chain of 20 stitches.
2. Single crochet in each of the stitch across the chain. Make chain of one then turn.
3. Make single crochet in each of the stitch across the row. Make chain of one then turn.
4. Continue by repeating step 3 until the piece measures about 7 inches in length.
5. Fold the piece in half, and slip stitch (st) the sides together to create a seam, leaving a hole for the thumb.
6. Turn the mittens right side out.

To create the thumb hole:

7. Count four stitches from the mitten's side, and use a stitch marker to indicate the fifth stitch.
8. Slip stitch (st) the mitten's edge to the designated stitch.
9. Around the thumb hole, make chain of one and single crochet in each stitch.
10. Make chain of one and single crochet one more around the thumb hole in each stitch.
11. The round is connected using a slip stitch (st), and any loose ends are then woven in.
12. To make the second mitten, keep going by repeating the instructions above.

Lorena Jackson

Crochet Cap

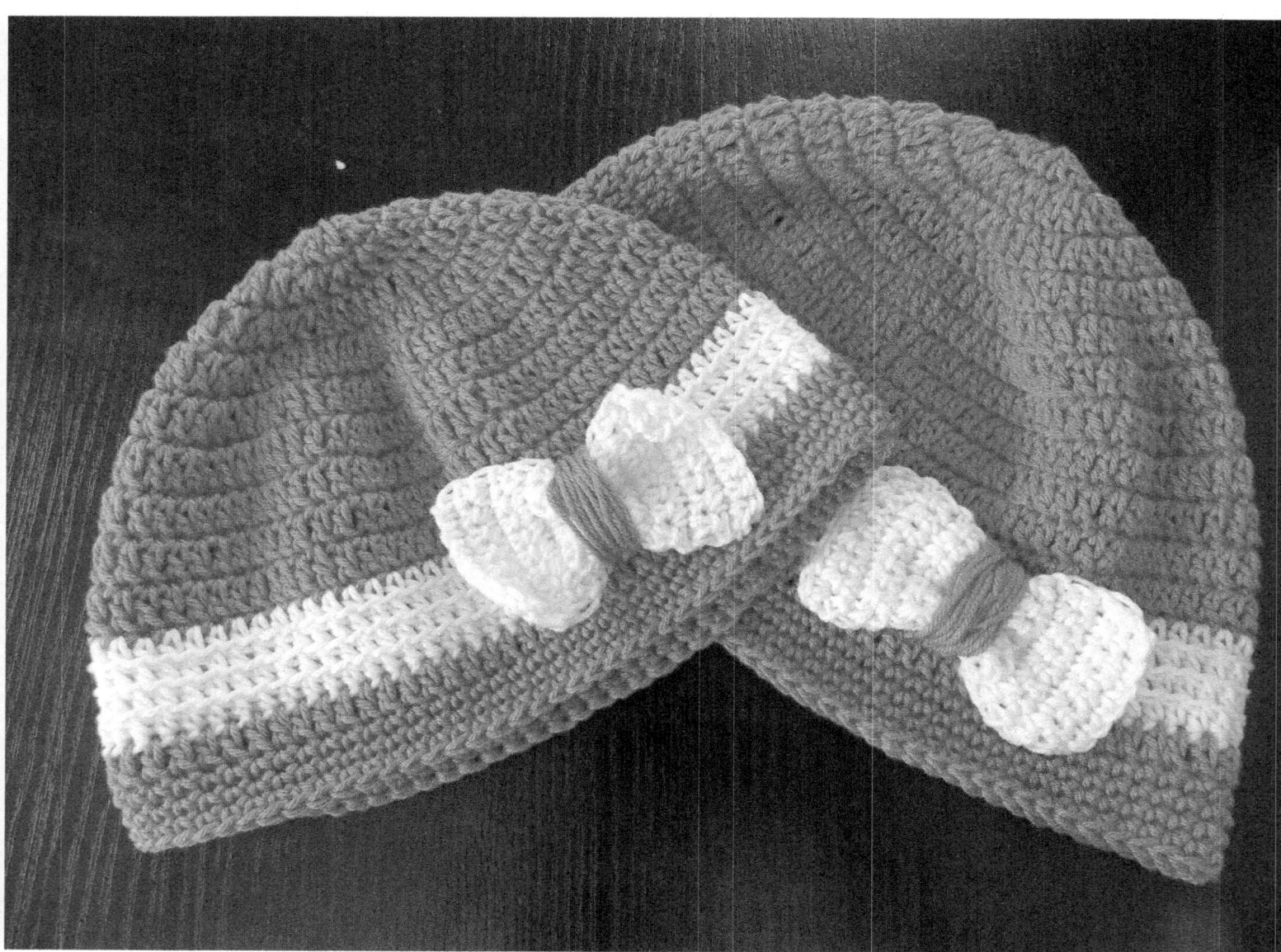

Supplies:

- Pick a (any color) worsted weight yarn.
- Take a H/5mm sized crochet hook.
- Scissors
- Tapestry needle

Directions:

1. To begin, create a magic circle and then make chain of two stitches. Proceed to make ten double crochet stitches into the circle, and then connect the last stitch to the 1st dc using a slip stitch (sl st). (10 stitches)
2. Make chain of two stitches and make two dc stitches into every stitch around. Connect the stitch to the 1st double crochet's top using a slip stitch (st). (20 stitches)
3. Make chain of two stitches and make one dc stitch into the following stitch, followed by two dc stitches into the subsequent stitch. Continue by repeating this pattern throughout the round. Connect the stitch to the 1st double crochet's top using a slip stitch (st). (30 stitches)
4. Make chain of two stitches and make one dc stitch into each of the adjacent two stitches, followed by two dc stitches into the subsequent stitch. Continue by repeating this pattern throughout the round. Connect the stitch to the 1st double crochet's top using a slip stitch (st). (40 stitches)
5. Make chain of two stitches and make one dc stitch into each of the adjacent three stitches, followed by two dc stitches into the subsequent stitch. Continue by repeating this pattern throughout the round. Connect the end using a slip stitch (st) to the 1st double crochet's top. (50 stitches)
6. Make chain of two stitches and work 1 double crochet on each stitch around for rounds six through fifteen. A slip stitch (st) is used to connect the stitch to the top of the 1st stitch of double crochet. (Fifty stitches)
7. Your yarn's loose ends should be woven after being cut off..

Lorena Jackson

Crochet Shawl

Supplies:

- Worsted weight yarn in the color of your liking
- Take a H/5mm sized crochet hook
- Scissors
- Tapestry needle

Crochet for Beginners

Directions:

This shawl is worked from the top down.

1. Chain 6.
2. Begin row 1 by making a double crochet stitch into that 4th chain from your crochet's hook. Then connect another dc stitch into each of the adjacent 2 chains. Turn your work to continue. (3 stitches)
3. Chaining three counts as 1 double crochet (dc) in row 2. Then, work 2 double crochets into the stitch directly below the 1st, and one single crochet into the last stitch. your job around. Five stitches
4. To finish row 3, make chain of 3 (which is counted as 1 double crochet), work on a 1 double crochet in that 1st stitch, then perform 1 double crochet on each of the adjacent 2 stitches, again make 2 double crochet in that adjacent stitch, and 1 double crochet in that final stitch. your job around. Seven stitches
5. In row 4, make chain of 3 (which is counted as 1 dc), work 1 double crochet on the 1st stitch, then perform 2 double crochet on the stitch adjacent to it, then 1 double crochet on each of the remaining 4 stitches.
6. For row 5, make chain of 3 (which is counted as 1 dc), make one double crochet on the 1st stitch, create 1 double crochet on each of the adjacent 6 stitches, perform 2 double crochet on the adjacent stitch, and perform 1 double crochet on each of the last 2 stitches. Turn your work. (11 stitches)
7. Keep working in this manner, with 1 dc in each of the stitch, until the shawl reaches your desired size. You can add a finishing touch by incorporating an edging, such as a row of single crochet or picot stitches.
8. Fasten off the loose ends of your yarn and weave them.

You can customize this shawl by using different colors or types of yarn, adjusting the size, or adding embellishments such as fringe or tassels. Enjoy your new crochet shawl!

Lorena Jackson

Two Colored Crochet Bag

Supplies:

- Take a suitable yarn (worsted weight) in 2 different colors (A, and B)
- Take a H/5mm sized crochet hook
- Scissors
- Tapestry needle
- Two wooden or metal handles

Directions:

Body of the Bag:

1. Using color A, make chain of 35.
2. For the 1st row: Make one single crochet into the 2nd chain from your crochet's hook then into each chain across. Turn your work. (34 stitches)
3. Rows 2-10: Make chain of one stitch, make one single crochet into each stitch across. Turn your work.
4. Row 11: Change to color B. Make chain of one stitch, make one single crochet into each stitch across. Turn your work.
5. Rows 12-20: Make chain of one stitch, make one single crochet into each stitch across. Turn your work.
6. Continue by repeating the crocheted rows 11-20 until the body of the bag is the desired length.

Handle Straps:

7. Using color A, make chain of 60.
8. For the 1st row: Make one single crochet into the 2nd chain from your crochet's hook then into each chain across. Turn your work. (59 stitches)
9. Rows 2-4: Make chain of one stitch, make one single crochet into each stitch across. Turn your work.
10. Tie the loose ends. Continue by repeating for a 2nd handle strap.

Finishing:

11. With the right sides facing each other, fold the bag in half and stitch the sides while leaving the top open.
12. Attach the handle straps to the bag by sewing them onto the top edge of each side of the bag.
13. Attach the wooden or metal handles to the bag by sliding them through those loops of the handle straps.
14. Weave in any remaining ends and trim the excess yarn.

Your multicolor crochet bag is now complete!

Lorena Jackson

Crochet Cardigan

Supplies:

- Pick a suitable yarn (worsted weight) in any color of your liking
- Take a H/5mm sized crochet hook
- Scissors
- Tapestry needle
- Buttons (optional)

Directions:

Back:

1. Make chain of 54.
2. **For the 1st row:** Make 1 double crochet in that 3rd chain from your crochet's hook then into each chain across. Turn your work. (52 stitches)
3. **Rows 2-5:** Make chain of two stitches then make one double crochet on each stitch across. Turn your work.
4. **Rows 6-8:** Make chain of two stitches then make one double crochet on each stitch across. Turn your work.
5. **Rows 9-12:** Make chain of two stitches then make one double crochet on each stitch across. Turn your work.
6. Continue by repeating the crocheted rows 6-12 until the back measures your desired length.
7. Tie the loose ends.

Left Front:

8. Make chain of 27
9. **For the 1st row:** Make one dc in the 3rd chain from your crochet hook then into each chain across. Turn your work. (25 stitches)
10. **Rows 2-5:** Make chain of two stitches then make one double crochet on each stitch across. Turn your work.
11. **Rows 6-8:** Make chain of two stitches then make one double crochet on each stitch across. Turn your work.
12. **Rows 9-12:** Make chain of two stitches then make one double crochet on each stitch across. Turn your work.
13. Continue by repeating the crocheted rows 6-12 until the left front measures half the length of the back.
14. Tie the loose ends

Right Front:

15. Chain 27.

16. **For the 1st row:** Make one dc in the 3rd chain from your crochet's hook then into each chain across. Turn your work. (25 stitches)
17. **Rows 2-5:** Make chain of two stitches then make one double crochet on each stitch across. Turn your work.
18. **Rows 6-8:** Make chain of two stitches then make one double crochet on each stitch across. Turn your work.
19. **Rows 9-12:** Make chain of two stitches then make one double crochet on each stitch across. Turn your work.
20. Continue by repeating the crocheted rows 6-12 until the right front measures half the length of the back.
21. Tie the loose ends

Sleeves (Make 2):

22. Make chain of 26.
23. **For the 1st row:** Make one dc in the 3rd chain from your crochet's hook then into each chain across. Turn your work. (24 stitches)
24. **Rows 2-5:** Make chain of two stitches then make one double crochet on each stitch across. Turn your work.
25. **Rows 6-8:** Make chain of two stitches then make one double crochet on each stitch across. Turn your work.
26. **Rows 9-12:** Make chain of two stitches then make one double crochet on each stitch across. Turn your work.
27. Continue by repeating the crocheted rows 6-12 until the sleeve measures your desired length.
28. Tie the loose ends

Assembly:

29. Sew the shoulder seams together.
30. Sew the sleeves to the body.
31. Sew the side seams together.
32. Add buttons if desired.

Your two-color crochet cardigan is now complete!

Crochet for Beginners

Colorful Crochet Socks:

Supplies:

- Multicolored worsted weight yarn
- Take a G or H sized crochet hook
- Yarn needle
- Scissors

Directions:

This pattern is suitable for a women's size about 9 feet.

Toe:

1. With your 1st colour of yarn, create a circle using the magic ring technique.
2. 6 single crochets in a circle in the 1st round.
3. For the 2nd round: To create up to 12 stitches, perform two single crochets in each knot around.
4. For the 3rd round: Work two single crochets in each subsequent slip stitch (st) and one single crochet in each succeeding st around. (18)
5. Round 4: Around, make two single crochet in each following slip stitch (st) and one single crochet in each succeeding two stitches. (24)
6. For the 5th round: Work two single crochets in each following slip stitch (st) and one single crochet every three stitches around. (30)
7. For the 6th round: Work one single crochet every four stitches, followed by two single crochets every slip stitch (st), all around. (36)
8. For the 7th round: Make one single crochet in succeeding 5 st, two single crochet in succeeding slip stitch (st) around. (42)
9. For the 8th round: Make one single crochet in succeeding 6 st, two single crochet in succeeding slip stitch (st) around. (48)
10. For the 9th round: Make one single crochet in succeeding 7 st, two single crochet in succeeding slip stitch (st) around. (54)
11. For the 10th round: Make one single crochet in succeeding 8 st, two single crochet in succeeding slip stitch (st) around. (60)

Foot:

12. From here on, make in rounds without increasing.
13. Round 11-24: 1 single crochet in each of the stitch (st) around.
14. Switch colors every 3 rounds or as desired.

Heel:

15. Using a different color of yarn, make the heel in rows.
16. For the 1st row: Ch 1, turn then perform a single crochet in the adjacent 30 St. Leave the remaining 30 st.
17. Rows 2-16: Ch 1, turn then perform a single crochet in each single stitch (st) across.

Ankle:

18. Connect the two sides of the heel with slip stitch (st)es. Continue making in rounds with the ankle section.
19. Round 1-10: 1 single crochet in each of the stitch (st) around.
20. Switch colors every 3 rounds or as desired.

Cuff:

21. Make the cuff in a rib stitch pattern.
22. For the 1st round: Ch 1, turn then perform a single crochet in the adjacent st Dc in the adjacent single knot.
23. Sc in the adjacent single knot, dc in the adjacent stitch (st) around.
24. Round 2-5: Continue by repeating Round 1.

Fasten off the ends of the yarn and weave in any loose ends. Continue by repeating the pattern for the 2nd sock.

Lorena Jackson

Crochet Blanket

Supplies:

- Choose a worsted yarn in your favorite color
- Take a H/5mm sized crochet hook

Directions:

Foundation Row:

1. To create the width of your blanket, chain a number of stitches equal to 3 plus 2. Chain 110 stitches, for instance, if you want a blanket that is 36 inches wide (3 x 36 Plus 2).
2. For the 1st row: Single crochet into the second chain from the hook then into every chain across the row above.
3. Two chains then turn.
4. Double crochet in that 1st stitch of row two.
5. Double crochet in that adjacent stitch after leaving the one after the 1st chain. Repeat the row, going from * to *.
6. Two chains then turn.
7. Single crochet into the 1st stitch in row three.
8. In the chain-1 space from the row before, make chain of two stitches and single crochet. Continue going across the row by repeating from * to *, ending with a single crochet at the chain's top from the row before then turn.
9. Two chains then turn.
10. Repeat the crocheted rows 2 and 3 as necessary to make the blanket the desired length. Fasten off your yarn and weave in any loose ends to complete the blanket.

This pattern creates a simple yet pretty pattern of alternating double crochet and chain-1 gaps. You can modify the pattern by using different stitches or stitch combinations to create a different look.

Lorena Jackson

Crochet Dishcloth

Supplies:

- Pick (in a color of choice) a suitable yarn (worsted weight).
- Take a G or H sized crochet hook

Directions:

1. Chain 21 stitches.
2. For the 1st row: Single crochet in each chain starting in the second chain from the crochet hook across. Twenty single crochets
3. Make chain of one stitch, turn, and single crochet in each stitch across in row 2.
4. Row 2 of the crochet pattern should be repeated once more until the dishcloth is square (approximately 20 rows).
5. Finish by weaving in the ends.

Working a round of single crochet around the edges will give the dishcloth a border. Start at either corner and, working three single crochets in each corner, work around the dishcloth, placing one stitch in each chain and stitch space. To connect and complete, slip stitch (st) into the 1st single crochet. Integrate ends.

A basic, textured dishcloth made with this pattern is excellent for cleaning dishes or doing other home chores. To make your dishcloth unique, try experimenting with different stitch patterns or colours.

Lorena Jackson

Crochet Headband

Supplies:

- Pick (in a color of choice) a suitable yarn (worsted weight).
- H or I sized crochet hook

Directions:

1. Make chain of 16 stitches.
2. Double crochet on each chain across Row 1 starting in the 3rd chain from the hook. In total make a total of 14 dc.
3. For the 2nd row: Make chain of two stitches then turn, and double crochet on each stitch all the way across.

4. For the 3rd row: Make chain of two stitches then turn, and work a double crochet on the 1st stitch, a bobble stitch in the thread adjacent to it, and another double crochet on the adjacent stitch. Repeat the row, going from * to *.
5. Make chain of two stitches then turn, and double crochet across each stitch in the 4th row.

   Make chain of two stitches then turn, and double crochet across each stitch in the 5th row.
6. Make chain of one stitch, turn, and single crochet across each stitch in the 6th row.
7. Make chain of one stitch, turn, and single crochet across each stitch in the 7th row.
8. Your yarn's loose ends should be weaved after being cut off.
9. Simply tie the headband over your head and alter the size as necessary to wear it.

Lorena Jackson

Crochet Granny Square

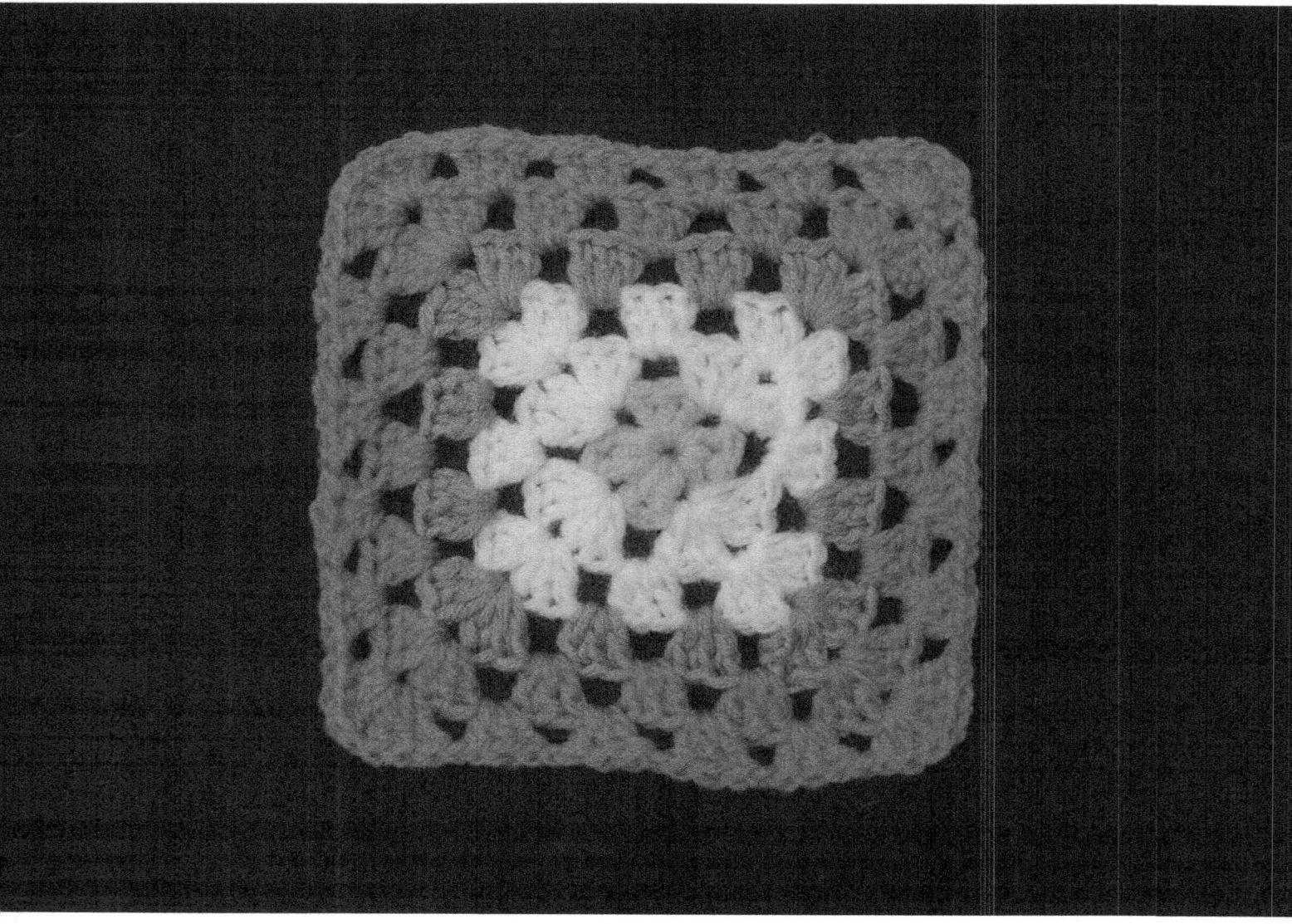

Supplies:

- Worsted weight yarn (you can choose any colors you like)
- H or I sized crochet hook

Directions:

For the 1st round:

1. Crochet a magic ring or you can make chain of 4 then make a slip stitch (st) to create a ring.
2. Make chain of 3 (which is counted as 1st double crochet, make 2 double crochet in that ring.
3. Make chain of two stitches then make three double crochet in that ring.
4. Make chain of two stitches then make three double crochet in that ring.
5. Make chain of two stitches then make three double crochet in that ring.
6. Make chain of two stitches then make a slip stitch (st) into the starting chain-3's top to connect.

For the 2nd round:

7. Slip stitch (st) into the 1st chain-2 gap.
8. Make chain of 3 then make 2 double crochet.
9. Make chain of one stitch, make three double crochet in that adjacent crochet chain-2 gap.
10. Make chain of two stitches then make three double crochet in that adjacent crochet chain-2 gap.
11. Make chain of one stitch, make three double crochet in that adjacent crochet chain-2 gap.
12. Make chain of two stitches and work three double crochets into the adjacent available chain-2 slot.
13. Make chain of one stitch and work three double crochets into the space left by the previous chain of crochet.
14. To connect, make chain of two stitches and slip stitch (st) into the 1st chain-3.

For the 3rd round:

15. In the 1st chain-2 gap, slip stitch (st).
16. Make 2 double crochets into the same chain-2 gap, considering the third chain as the 1st stitch of double crochet.
17. Make one chain, then three double crochets into the adjacent available chain-1 slot.
18. Make one chain, then three double crochets into the adjacent available chain-2 slot.
19. For three times repeat double crochet in that adjacent chain-2 gap, then make chain of two stitches again.
20. Make chain of one stitch, make three double crochet in that adjacent crochet chain-1 gap.
21. Make chain of one stitch, make three double crochet in that adjacent crochet chain-2 gap.
22. Make chain of two stitches then make three double crochet in that adjacent crochet chain-2 gap.
23. Make chain of one stitch, make three double crochet in that adjacent crochet chain-1 gap.
24. Make chain of two stitches then make a slip stitch (st) into the starting of chain-3's top to connect.

You can continue in the same way to make more rounds.

Crochet Beanie Cap Pattern

Supplies:

- Pick (in a color of choice) a suitable yarn (worsted weight).
- H or I sized crochet hook

Directions:

1. Create a magic ring in round 1 using crochet or, make chain of 4 and then perform a slip stitch to create a ring. Make 12 double crochets in the created ring in the second chain (which is counted as the 1st stitch of double crochet). To connect, slip stitch (st) to the 1st chain-2's top. (12 crochet doubles)
2. For the 2nd round: Double crochet twice into each stitch starting with a chain of two. To connect, slip stitch (st) to the 1st chain-2's top. Double crochet, 24
3. For the 3rd round: Make chain of two stitches; in the 1st stitch, work 2 double crochets; in the adjacent stitch, work 1 double crochet. Repeat from * to * in order to complete this round. To connect, slip stitch (st) to the 1st chain-2's top. (1 double crochet = 36)
4. For the 4th round: Make chain of two stitches; in the 1st stitch, make 2 double crochets; in the adjacent two stitches, make 1 double crochet. Repeat from * to * in order to complete this round. To connect, slip stitch (st) to the 1st chain-2's top. Double crochet, 48
5. Rounds five through ten: Make chain of two stitches then double crochet on each stitch all around. To connect, slip stitch (st) to the 1st chain-2's top. Double crochet, 48
6. Round 11: Single crochet in each stitch around, beginning with a chain of one stitch. To connect, add a slip stitch (st) to the 1st stitch of the chain. (48 crochet stitches)
7. 12th round: Chain 1, single crochet in 1st stitch, Chain 1, leave adjacent stitch. Repeat from * to * in order to complete this round. To connect, add a slip stitch (st) to the 1st stitch of the chain.
8. For the 13th round: Chain 1, perform one single crochet in the 1st space created by that chain 1, then single crochet in the stitch directly

below. Repeat from * to * in order to complete this round. To connect, add a slip stitch (st) to the 1st stitch of the chain.
9. Repeat Rounds 13 in Rounds 14 through 15 to continue.
10. Finish by weaving in the ends.

You can adjust the size of the beanie by adding or removing rounds. You can also experiment with different stitches, such as the half-double crochet or the treble crochet, to create different textures. You can also add a pom-pom or tassel to the top of the beanie for extra flair.

Lorena Jackson

Crochet Griddle Stitch Scarf Pattern

The Griddle Stitch is a fun textured stitch that works up quickly and creates a cozy, warm fabric. Here's a simple crochet Griddle Stitch Scarf pattern that you can try:

Crochet for Beginners

Supplies:

- Pick (in a color of choice) a suitable yarn (worsted weight).
- I or J sized crochet hook

Directions:

1. Depending on the width you desire for your scarf, chain a number of two stitches plus 1. Make a chain of twenty seven stitches, for instance, if you want a scarf that is about 6 inches wide.
2. In the fourth chain in row one from your hook, make a double crochet. Double crochet on the adjacent chain over, then single crochet in the adjacent chain. Continue going across the row from * to *, ending at double crochet on the final chain.
3. For the 2nd row: Chain 1, turn, work a single crochet in the adjacent stitch, followed by a double crochet on the adjacent stitch. Continue going across the row going from * to *, ending at a double crochet on the chain then turn.
4. Repeat row 2 of the crochet pattern until the scarf is the desired length, and then finish with a row on the wrong side.
5. Simple border: You can single crochet all around the scarf to produce a border. By cutting lengths of yarn and sewing them to the ends of the scarf, you may also add fringe.
6. Finish by weaving in the ends.

You can experiment with different color combinations to create a unique look. You can also adjust the length and width of the scarf to suit your preferences.

Lorena Jackson

Baby Crochet Blanket Pattern

Supplies:

- Worsted weight yarn in 3 different colors (you can choose any color combination you like)
- Take a G or H sized crochet hook

Crochet for Beginners

Directions:

1. With color A, chain 105.
2. For the 1st row: Make three double crochets starting on the 4th chain from your crochet hook. Make three double crochets in the next chain after leaving two chains. Continue going across the row from * to *, ending with 2 double crochet on the final chain. Turn your work.
3. For the 2nd row: Make chain of 3, then in the space between the double crochet clusters from For the 1st row, make three double crochet. In the space between the double crochet clusters in the row before, make three more double crochets. Continue repeating throughout the row from * to *, stopping with a 1 double crochet at the beginning of the turning chain. Turn your work.
4. Repeat crochet row 2 for rows three through five, switching to colour B at the start of row five.
5. Repeat crochet row 2 for rows six through eight, switching to colour C at the start of row eight.
6. Repeat crochet row 2 for rows 9 through 11, switching to colour A at the start of row 11.
7. Crochet rows 2 through 11 once more until the blanket is the desired length, and then finish with 3 rows in colour A.
8. Simple border: You can single crochet all around the blanket to produce a border. If you'd like, you can also add a border that is more aesthetically pleasing, such a scalloped edge.
9. Finish by weaving in the ends.

Crochet Bracelet Pattern

Supplies:

- Crochet cotton thread in the color of your liking
- 2.5 or 3 mm sized crochet hook
- Sewing needle
- Small button or bead for the closure

Directions:

1. Chain as many stitches as will comfortably fit around your wrist to begin. You can chain about 30-35 stitches for a typical wrist size. To create a ring, sew the final chain to the 1st chain. Don't twist the chain, please.

2. Single crochet in each chain around after the 1st one. It should be attached to the 1st single crochet using a slip stitch (st).
3. Single crochet in each single crochet around after making one chain. It should be attached to the 1st single crochet using a slip stitch (st).
4. Up until the bracelet reaches the desired width, repeat step 3 as necessary. To make sure the bracelet has a comfortable fit, you can occasionally try it on.
5. Cut the ends and thread them in.
6. Sew on a button to add a closure..

Your crochet bracelet is now ready to wear! You can make multiple bracelets in different colors to match your outfits or give them as gifts to friends and family.

Crochet Gloves Pattern

Supplies:

- Worsted weight yarn in the color of your liking
- H or I sized crochet hook
- Stitch marker
- Yarn needle

Crochet for Beginners

Directions:

This pattern is for an adult-sized pair of gloves.

1. Glove Body:
2. Chain 22. To create a ring, sew it together using a slip stitch (st).
3. In each chain around, single crochet. The round's end should be marked with a stitch marker.
4. Single crochet around in each subsequent single crochet. Repeat this process until the glove is the proper length from the base of your palm to the tip of your middle finger. To get an accurate fit, you can measure against your own hand.
5. Chain 6 after creating 6 single crochet stitches. Make 10 single crochet stitches after leaving 6 stitches. Chain 6. Make 6 single crochet stitches after leaving 6 stitches. It should be attached to the 1st single crochet using a slip stitch (st). The opening for the thumb will result from this.
6. In between each chain and every single crochet, single crochet. Repeat this process until the glove is the proper length from the base of your palm to the tip of your middle finger.
7. Your yarn's loose ends should be weaved after being cut off.
8. At the base of the thumb opening, connect the yarn.
9. Chain around and single crochet in each stitch. Repeat this process until the thumb is the appropriate length.
10. Your yarn's loose ends should be weaved after being cut off.
11. Repeat the aforementioned procedure to make the second glove.

Crochet Crop Top Pattern

Supplies:

- Pick worsted weight cotton yarn in the color of your liking
- Take a G or H sized crochet hook
- Yarn needle

Directions:

This pattern is for a size small/medium crop top.

Top Body:

1. Chain 67. Turn your work.
2. Double crochet on each chain starting with the 4th chain from your crochet hook. Turn your work.
3. Double crochet on the 3rd chain of each double crochet after that. Turn your work.
4. Repeat step 3 as necessary until the top's length from the bottom to just below the bust is the desired length. You can occasionally put it on to make sure it fits comfortably.
5. Ends should be cut off and weaved in..

Cups:

6. On one side of the upper body, connect the yarn to the top edge.
7. For each stitch across, double crochet. 3, spin the chain.
8. In the initial double crochet, make a double crochet. Leave the adjacent double crochet after the 1st chain. In the double crochet adjacent to it, double crochet. Leave the adjacent double crochet after the 1st chain. Repeat from * to * one more. In the final double crochet, double crochet. 3, spin the chain.
9. Repeat step 3 as necessary until the cup measures the desired height. You can sometimes try it on to make sure it comfortably covers your bust.
10. Cut the ends and thread them in.
11. Repeat the aforementioned procedure for the second cup.

Straps:

12. Connect the yarn to one cup's top edge.
13. Double crochet across each stitch after making a chain of three. Turn your work.

14. Double crochet on the 3rd chain of each double crochet after that. Turn your work.
15. Repeat step 3 as necessary until the strap is the desired length. You can occasionally put it on to make sure it fits your shoulder comfortably.
16. Cut the ends and thread them in.
17. Repeat the aforementioned method once more for the second strap..

Your crochet crop top is now ready to wear! You can make multiple tops in different colors to match your outfits or give them as gifts to friends and family.

Crochet Cowl Pattern

Supplies:

- Bulky weight yarn in the color of your liking
- Crochet hook (size N or P)
- Yarn needle

Directions:

This pattern is for an adult-sized cowl.

1. To create a ring, slip stitch (st) 80 chains together.

2. Double crochet on each chain around after the second chain. It should be attached to the 1st stitch of double crochet at the top using a slip stitch (st).

3. Double crochet on the back loop of each double crochet around after the second chain. It should be attached to the 1st stitch of double crochet at the top using a slip stitch (st).

4. Repeat step 3 as necessary until the cowl is the desired length. You can occasionally put it on to make sure it feels well around your neck.

5. Cut the ends and thread them in.

Your crochet cowl is now ready to wear! You can make multiple cowls in different colors and textures to match your outfits or give them as gifts to friends and family.

Chapter 10: FAQ

What is crocheting?

Crocheting is a needlework technique that involves using a hook and yarn or thread to create fabric.

What materials do I need to start crocheting?

To start crocheting, you will need a yarn, different sizes of hooks, and a pattern or Directions.

Is there are a variety of hooks you can use to crochet?

There are several types of crochet hooks, including aluminum, plastic, bamboo, and steel. They also come in different sizes, with the size of your crochet's hook depending on the thickness of the yarn.

What types of yarn are best for crocheting?

The type of crochet yarn you choose will depend on the project you are working on. Some common types of yarn include acrylic, wool, cotton, and blends of these fibers.

How do I read a crochet pattern?

Crochet patterns use a combination of symbols and abbreviations to describe the stitches and techniques used in a project. To read a pattern, you will need to become familiar with these symbols and abbreviations.

What are some common crochet projects for beginners?

Some common crochet projects for beginners include scarves, hats, and dishcloths.

How can I improve my crocheting skills?

Practice is key when it comes to improving your crocheting skills. You can also take classes or watch online tutorials to learn new techniques and stitches.

What are some resources for crocheters?

There are many online resources available for crocheters, including blogs, forums, and online communities. You can also find books, magazines, and classes to help improve your skills.

Conclusion

Crocheting is a fun and rewarding craft that can be enjoyed by anyone, regardless of skill level. A crochet for beginners book can provide you with the guidance and instruction you need to get started, whether you're looking to make cozy blankets and scarves, cute amigurumi toys, or trendy accessories like hats and bags. With the help of this crochet for beginners book, you can learn the basics of crocheting, from the different types of stitches to the various yarns and hooks available. You'll also have the opportunity to practice your skills with beginner-friendly patterns that are both fun and functional. In addition to being a fun and creative outlet, crocheting can also be a relaxing and stress-reducing activity. By focusing on the rhythm and flow of your stitches, you can enjoy a meditative and calming experience that can help you unwind after a long day. Overall, if you're interested to know how to crochet, this book is a great resource to have on hand. So grab your crochet hook and yarn, get ready to start creating some beautiful and unique crochet projects!

Made in the USA
Las Vegas, NV
22 April 2023

70967048R00057